TYLER PERRY

Other titles in the series **African-American Icons**

BEYONCÉ
A Biography of a Legendary Singer
ISBN 978-0-7660-4230-8

CHRIS ROCK
A Biography of a Comic Genius
ISBN 978-0-7660-4229-2

JAY-Z
A Biography of a Hip-Hop Icon
ISBN 978-0-7660-4232-2

JENNIFER HUDSON
A Biography of an American Music Idol
ISBN 978-0-7660-4233-9

SEAN "DIDDY" COMBS
A Biography of a Music Mogul
ISBN 978-0-7660-4296-4

TYLER PERRY

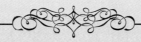

A Biography of a Movie Mogul

Marty Gitlin

 Enslow Publishers, Inc.
40 Industrial Road
Box 398
Berkeley Heights, NJ 07922
USA
http://www.enslow.com

Library of Congress Cataloging-in-Publication Data

Gitlin, Marty.
  Tyler Perry : a biography of a movie mogul / Marty Gitlin.
      pages cm. — (African-American icons)
  Includes bibliographical references and index.
  Summary: "Explores the life of Tyler Perry, including his difficult childhood and
troubled family life, his rise from a struggling playwright to a movie mogul, the
controversy over his works, and his status as an entertainment icon"
—Provided by publisher.
  ISBN 978-0-7660-4241-4
  1. Perry, Tyler—Juvenile literature. 2. African American motion picture producers and
directors—Juvenile literature. 3. African American authors—Biography—Juvenile
literature. I. Title.
  PN1998.3.P4575G55 2014
  791.4302'8092—dc23
  [B]
                              2013012730
Future editions:
Paperback ISBN: 978-1-4644-0425-2
EPUB ISBN: 978-1-4645-1232-2
Single-User PDF ISBN: 978-1-4646-1232-9
Multi-User PDF ISBN: 978-0-7660-5864-4

Printed in the United States of America
112013 Lake Book Manufacturing, Inc., Melrose Park, IL
10 9 8 7 6 5 4 3 2 1

To Our Readers: We have done our best to make sure all Internet addresses in this
book were active and appropriate when we went to press. However, the author and
the publisher have no control over and assume no liability for the material available
on those Internet sites or on other Web sites they may link to. Any comments or
suggestions can be sent by e-mail to comments@enslow.com or to the address on
the back cover.

♻ Enslow Publishers, Inc., is committed to printing our books on recycled paper. The
paper in every book contains 10% to 30% post-consumer waste (PCW). The cover board
on the outside of each book contains 100% PCW. Our goal is to do our part to help
young people and the environment too!

Cover Illustration: AP Images / Charles Sykes.

CONTENTS

Chapter 1

FORGIVING, NOT FORGETTING

Two paths lay before Emmitt Perry, Jr. He was in his early twenties and standing at the crossroads.

He could let his anger control his emotions and prevent him from reaching his potential. Or, he could turn his rage into compassion and forge a new and productive life.

One might understand if he stumbled down the road of self-destruction. There was much to overcome. He had been horribly abused by his father, who had beaten him savagely and without cause for many years.

He had been sexually molested as a child by both men and women. Few could blame him if he wallowed in misery and resentment.

But Perry chose the path of forgiveness. He could not forget the terrible cruelty of those who mistreated him. It was too fresh in his mind. He could still feel the pain and shame. So he decided to use those agonizing experiences for emotional healing and professional fulfillment.

He had made the first symbolic gesture years earlier by separating himself from his father, Emmitt Perry, Sr. The younger Perry did not want to share the same first name as his father. At age sixteen, he changed his name to Tyler.

Several years passed. Despite the new name, Tyler Perry felt the same anger as Emmitt Perry, Jr. He needed an outlet for the bitterness that remained inside of him. It was fortunate that he happened to flip on the television one fateful day in his early twenties. He began listening to iconic talk show host Oprah Winfrey. He heard a guest explain the positive emotional effects of writing.

Something inside Perry became unleashed. He began to believe he could heal by expressing his feelings through the power of the pen. At the age of twenty-two, he started writing a series of letters to himself. He sought liberation from all his anger.

Perry did not only remember the thrashings at the hands of his father and the sexual abuse that had haunted him to that day. He also recalled the few pleasant moments of his youth, such as when his mother gave him refuge from his fear by taking him to church. It was there he felt a sense of peace and contentment. As he embarked on taking personal responsibility for his therapy, he embraced a strong belief in God and the power of religion. It would help him through the darkest periods of young adulthood.

The words of wisdom he wrote to himself became the basis of his first play, a musical appropriately titled *I Know I've Been Changed.* The work was not only an attempt to make money and plant the seeds for a career. It also served as a message of hope for others who had been abused. Perry felt that relieving the emotional agony of those who shared his experiences would aid him in relieving his own pain. He explained his thoughts in a 2009 interview with *Essence Magazine.* "Once a bad thing has happened to you, you can be completely ashamed of it and it can destroy you, or you can take the power out of it by using it as a teaching tool to help others," he said.

The message of his play centered on forgiveness and self-respect. It also explored other issues, such as child abuse. It provided therapy for Perry, but it did not provide badly needed financial help—at least not at first. In 1990, Perry moved from New Orleans, Louisiana, to Atlanta, Georgia, where he spent his life savings of $12,000 earned from various low-paying jobs to finance the play.

He did not just put all his money into *I Know I've Been Changed*—he invested his heart and soul. He composed the music, designed the sets, and starred onstage when it finally debuted in a community theater two years later. Every night, fewer patrons showed up. He lived out of his car for three months in an attempt to keep the show alive. But it was to no avail. The play was a critical and financial flop.

Perry remained undaunted. He refused to accept failure. He believed in his talent. He toiled over the next six years to make the play stronger. It reappeared at the House of Blues in Atlanta in 1998. He promoted it tirelessly within the black community. It was the last hope for *I Know I've Been Changed*.

The result was a smash hit. The play sold out on opening night. The crowds that besieged the venue forced it into the larger Fox Theater. Soon, the play was being produced in other major American cities, including New York.

Perry did not look in the mirror to find the reason for his success. He credited God, whom he believed had granted him good fortune for forgiving his father.

Perry would consider the wealth, fame, and satisfaction a blessing from above for the rest of his career.

His religious awakening and desire to continue helping those who had been abused led him to his next project in 1999, a gospel-driven musical titled *Woman, Thou Art Loosed.* Perry adapted the work from a book written by Texas evangelist T. D. Jakes. It revolved around a woman seeking to recover from mistreatment, drug addiction, and poverty. Perry would never have to worry about poverty again. The play grossed $5 million.

He was just warming up. His next work launched a character with whom he would be identified for years to come. The creation of a grandmotherly figure named Mabel "Madea" Simmons was based on his mother and several other women in his life. There was something unique about how she was presented— Perry played the role himself as he donned a wig, a polka-dot dress, and thick glasses.

The fictional character commonly referred to as Madea, who first appeared in the 2000 play *I Can Do Bad All by Myself,* has been a fixture in Perry productions for more than a decade. The gun-toting grandma is noted for her toughness, profane language, and vengeful nature. She threatens violence against those she believes have wronged the people she loves. Her lack of education becomes apparent when she mispronounces words. She has found herself in court, anger management classes, and even jail. But she is motivated only by her affection for family and friends. She wants to create what she perceives is a better society. She is the moral compass in all the Perry works in which she appears.

Perry conceived of the name Madea by combining the words "mama" and "dear." She is one of the most controversial figures in the history of African-American media. Some critics have complained that she is a negative stereotype of African Americans. They claim her ignorance and violent tendencies are a poor reflection on African-American women and black people in general. They have criticized African Americans who have flocked to theaters to watch Madea and increased the ratings of television shows in which she has been cast.

Perry has countered with anger and resentment. He has defended patrons of his plays and films starring Madea. He believes that nobody has the right to tell his fans what to watch or condemn their taste in entertainment. His supporters have offered that Perry is simply seeking to evoke laughter while providing good lessons in morality. They stress that his work is not intended to be a statement about African-American life.

Even his harshest critics praise Perry for his business savvy. He has turned his talent into a financial empire. His ability as an actor, director, writer, and producer has led him to unprecedented success. *Forbes* magazine claimed he earned $130 million in a one-year period beginning in May 2010. This made him the highest-paid entertainer in the United States during that time.

Early in his career, Perry could never have imagined such achievements while sleeping in his car and living in shoddy apartments in Atlanta. He found his niche through the Madea character, which black audiences embraced. He featured her in several plays in the early 2000s, including the highly popular *Diary of a Mad Black Woman* (2001), *Madea's Family Reunion* (2002), and *Madea's Class Reunion* (2003). Perry toured with his shows throughout the country. He estimated in 2005 that one production attracted thirty-five thousand patrons in a week.

It is no wonder Perry sought to bring Madea to the big screen. *Diary of a Mad Black Woman* debuted on film in 2005. Perry showed his versatility by appearing as three different characters in the movie, which earned more than $50 million. Perry had proven the potential of urban African-American comedies.

Hollywood quickly jumped on the Perry band-wagon. Perry did not need to create new productions.

The success of *Diary of a Mad Black Woman* convinced movie studios that they could profit from transforming his plays into movies. Film adaptations of *Madea's Family Reunion* (2006) and *I Can Do Bad All by Myself* (2009) followed.

By that time, Perry had taken Madea into a new world. In 2006, he published his best-selling book *Don't Make a Black Woman Take Off Her Earrings: Madea's Uninhibited Commentaries on Love and Life.* The book expressed his views on a variety of subjects. At its heart a self-help book, it promoted his belief in the importance of faith and forgiveness.

It seemed Perry would be forever tied to the character he brought to life as a writer and actor. But he proved he did not need Madea to create popular entertainment. In 2006, he launched *House of Payne,* his first television sitcom appearing on WTBS. He directed the program about a multigenerational black family. Perry showed that he did not have to act in one of his productions to enjoy success. The dramatic scenes and situations mixed in with the comedy proved that Perry did not rely strictly on humor to attract TV viewers. Madea appeared infrequently on the show.

While *House of Payne* was gaining an audience, Perry continued to prove his versatility as he threw himself into every aspect of the filmmaking process.

It seemed that patrons, especially urban African-American women, could not wait until his next release. His movies packed theaters. In 2007, he wrote, directed, and produced *Why Did I Get Married?* The movie opened at number one in the box office and earned $21.4 million on its first weekend. His 2008 films *Meet the Browns* and *The Family That Preys* combined to take in more than $57 million.

By that time, cable television network TBS had become convinced that Perry's television shows could result in huge ratings. The success of *House of Payne* motivated TBS to launch a TV adaptation of *Meet the Browns*, which he also wrote, directed, and produced. Perry was not done transforming his movies into sitcoms. In 2011, TBS debuted *Tyler Perry's For Better or Worse*, based on *Why Did I Get Married?* and its sequel *Why Did I Get Married Too?*

Barely a decade had passed since Perry was living out of his car in Atlanta. He was now among the richest entertainers in America. Wealth and fame had changed his lifestyle, but it had not changed him. His faith remained as strong as ever. He continued to place moral messages into his work. He even sought to establish a positive relationship with his father, the man who had beaten him repeatedly as a child.

Perry would never forget the almost unbearable circumstances in which he was raised. He yearned to help others, especially young African Americans who had been treated badly. Stories arose about his charity work, though he never bragged about it or sought publicity.

In the summer of 2009, a group of sixty-five African-American children from a day camp was barred from a suburban Philadelphia swim club. Perry responded by sponsoring a trip for them to Walt Disney World. He explained his motivation in a statement published on the CNN Web site. "This is awful, and for anyone that has grown up in the inner city, you know that one small act of kindness can change your life," he said. "I want them to know that for every act of evil that a few people will throw at you, there are millions more who will do something kind for them."

Meanwhile, millions more trekked to the theaters to watch new Perry movies as the first decade of the twenty-first century neared its end. He brought back the characters that launched him to stardom in *Madea Goes to Jail*, which opened at number one in the box office in 2009. His seventh Madea movie—*Madea's Big Happy Family*—proved to be a hit in 2011.

His most critically acclaimed film of the era was *Precious*, for which he and Oprah Winfrey served as coproducers. The film centered on an abused, obese sixteen-year-old African-American girl struggling to survive emotionally in the Harlem section of New York City. It was a theme that hit close to home for Perry. Even though he had not been plagued by obesity as a child, and he was raised hundreds of miles from New York, he knew all about abuse.

In a strange way, it was what made him the man he had become. Perry never would have been given the choice of taking the right path in life had he not been forced down the wrong path in his youth. Asked by Winfrey what the older Tyler Perry owes the younger one, he explained that the adult owes the child his life.

"I think that [the younger Perry] had to endure so much and had no recourse," he said. "He had no help. He just had to walk through it. He gave birth to the man I am. I owe him to live the best life I can. I owe him to be the best father that I will be someday. I owe him to use my life and my words and my work to encourage, to inspire . . . "[1]

Little could he have imagined as he grew up in New Orleans that he would become an inspiration to millions. During that terrible time, he was just trying to survive.

Chapter 2

SURVIVING MISERY

Emmitt Perry, Jr., was born on September 13, 1969. There were times during his youth that he wished he had never been born at all.

Father Emmitt, Sr., and mother Maxine raised him along with three siblings in a poor section of New Orleans. Persistent violence and incidents of sexual abuse marked his childhood.

Physical cruelty is often passed down through generations. Such was the case in the Perry family tree. Tyler learned later in life that his father had also been abused as a child. A woman too young and incapable of handling the responsibility of motherhood raised the elder Perry.

In an interview with talk show host Piers Morgan, Tyler Perry spoke about the upbringing of his father, who was found at the age of two in a drainage ditch by a white man. "He was brought to a 14 year-old woman named May to raise," Perry said. "And everything that she knew to do to get these children to behave was to beat them. And she would tie them in a potato sack, hang them in a tree and she would beat them."

Emmitt Perry took the same approach to discipline, though he often violently beat his son for no reason. Tyler recalled one thrashing vividly. While his mother was away, his drunken father cornered him in his room. His father smacked him repeatedly with a vacuum cleaner cord. The beating raised five huge welts on his skin.

The boy waited for his father to fall asleep before racing to the home of Aunt Jerry. To her horror, she lifted his shirt to discover the wounds. She picked up a gun and walked with a purpose to the Perry home, where she met Emmitt on the sidewalk. She pointed the gun at his head. Aunt Jerry's husband arrived to remove the gun from her hands. However, she later informed Maxine that she would never again allow her nephew to be left alone with his father.

Though Tyler accompanied Jerry everywhere she went, he could not avoid terrible moments with Emmitt, Sr. On one occasion, he was given the task of changing a tire. His father screamed and swore at his son, who tried in vain to remove the rusted bolts. After failing to loosen the bolts himself, Emmitt tackled the boy and hit him repeatedly. The child hung on so hard to a chain-link fence during the beating that his hand began to bleed. He then blacked out for three days.

Emmitt even used psychological tricks as an excuse to beat Tyler. He knew that Tyler, like most other children, loved cookies. He would buy cookies and place them atop the refrigerator. When Emmitt discovered that his son had eaten the cookies, he would beat him.

Tyler lived in such fear that he saw no point in living. One day, in a desperate cry for help, Tyler slit his wrists in a suicide attempt. He was fortunate that he did not slit them deeply enough to achieve his goal.

There was only one occasional relief from his torturous life, as he explained on *The Oprah Winfrey Show* in 2010. "My mother was truly my saving grace, because she would take me to church with her," he said. "I would see my mother smiling in the choir, and I wanted to know this God that made her so happy.

If I had not had that faith in my life, I don't know where I would be right now."

The inspiration he received from Sunday church services would forever remain with him. He felt inspired to worship with others experiencing pain in their lives. He knew they too were gaining therapy for their souls.

"There's nothing like the black church, there's nothing like it in America," he said in a feature on his life on the Biography Channel. "To feel the power of God in this place and to hear all these people who are going through all kinds of things get a release was really powerful for me."[1]

Tyler accompanied Maxine on other errands as well, such as to the beauty shop and laundry. He claimed later in life that he learned a great deal about women listening closely to their conversations. The experiences and understanding would eventually help him create depth in purpose and personality in his female characters.

He also sought refuge in private moments. He enjoyed reading, writing, and art. He was so talented at drawing that at the age of twelve, he was designing additions to Emmitt's carpentry and home-building business. He earned forty dollars a drawing but could not gain the appreciation of his father. Tyler complained later in life that Emmitt did not like his artistic side or the fact that he received excellent grades in school.

The Perry family lacked a sense of togetherness. They did not eat meals together, rarely went on excursions, or even attended movies. The world of film and theater in which Tyler would later emerge as a huge success was foreign to him as a boy. He recalled seeing just one movie during his childhood. He was taken to see *The Wiz*, an African-American musical based on the iconic film *The Wizard of Oz*. Tyler was so inspired by the experience that he danced all the way home.

Tyler did escape through television. He loved watching reruns of the funny 1960s sitcom *Gilligan's Island*, which featured silly humor revolving around seven castaways stuck on a desert island. He believed as a small child that the characters were living inside his TV. He wanted to unscrew the back of his set to see if he could see them, but he knew that would incur the wrath of his father.

Though he was still young, he later developed sophisticated taste in television programming and an appreciation for creative talent. He loved shows written by Norman Lear, who revolutionized the sitcom by focusing on social and political issues. Lear's breakthrough show, *All in the Family*, was arguably the most critically acclaimed sitcom in TV history.

It focused on social and political issues not discussed previously in fictional programming.

Real life was simply too agonizing for Tyler. His only other escape outside of TV when he was alone was through his imagination. He would visualize his mother or aunt taking him to the park, where he would be running, playing, and enjoying himself. When others were treating him badly, Tyler would picture a scene of freedom and happiness until the painful moments of reality were over.

Tyler was also a sickly child. He was stricken with severe asthma, which made it difficult for him to breathe. He was forced to go to the doctor every Tuesday for shots to control his allergies, but Emmitt showed no compassion. The problem intensified every summer, when the family would visit Emmitt's adoptive mother in the country. Emmitt hated that Tyler could not breathe well around the pollen and trees that were everywhere in that environment.

Emmitt's mother expressed dismay when she learned of her grandson's weekly doctor visits. She said there was nothing wrong with him and that paying a doctor was a waste of money. She claimed that he simply needed to rid himself of the germs on his body. One day, she interrupted his playing to soak him in a bathtub filled with ammonia.

A stronger mother figure might have pulled her children away from all the abuse. Maxine was a loving mother to Tyler, but she was not emotionally tough enough to fight back against her husband. She did try to escape with her children when Tyler was very young. She drove them to California, but Emmitt reported the car stolen, and she was arrested. Tyler recalled Emmitt beating Maxine throughout the long ride home.

"My mother wasn't like my aunt," Perry told Winfrey. "She was just very passive. She did not have that backbone to stand up for herself; she certainly couldn't stand up for me."

Tyler later tried to gain an understanding of his mother's actions by learning about her past. Her mother died when she was thirteen. At the tender age of seventeen, she married Emmitt, who took her to live in New Orleans. She did not know how to take care of herself or support herself financially. Despite the abuse she would take from her husband, her relatives would advise her to stay with him.

Tyler often wished she would leave Emmitt and take him with her. But he understood her hesitation as he got older. He explained his feelings to National Public Radio interviewer Terry Gross. "What was clear about it is that she had no way to support four children, and as bad as things were, as bad of a person as he could be, the man [was a] provider," he said. "The lights were never off. You know, we did have everything we wanted."

The beatings from his father would have been traumatic enough for any child. But Tyler was also forced to endure sexual abuse from adult men and women. He was fondled by a male neighbor while helping him build a birdhouse at the age of five or six. Two other men molested him, including a nurse and a member of his church congregation, who tried to justify his actions through passages from the Bible.

Tyler vividly recalled another disturbing incident at the age of ten in which he was sexually abused by the mother of his friend. The woman locked her son in the bathroom and tried to have sex with Tyler, who did not yet understand what sex was.

Emmitt was also involved in a similar traumatic experience for Tyler, who explained the disturbing incident in a feature on the online site *HelloBeautiful*. "I was about 8 or 9 years old," he began. "I had a crush on a little girl across the street. She would come over to my house and we would play. She was about 12 or 13. One day she stopped coming and when I asked her why, she told me that my father was touching her. I didn't believe her, so I talked her into staying one night. We were both asleep—she was in one bed and I was in another. I opened my eyes to see my father trying to touch her and her pushing him away."[2]

Tyler never believed he would reach adulthood. "I always thought I would die before I grew up," he later wrote on his Web site. He grew as angry as he was fearful as a teenager. He sought to distance himself from his father at age sixteen by changing his name from Emmitt, Jr., to Tyler. It was not a legal switch but rather a spontaneous one.

"One day, somebody asked me what my name was. I said Tyler," he explained on the Biography Channel. "I don't know where it came from. That was the name that popped in my head."

The name change was only a symbolic gesture. It alone did not improve his life. His father continued to beat him throughout his teenage years. The angry youth felt confused about his future, though he never believed that he would be abusive to others, as many children of abusive parents become. He felt that his religious upbringing would save him from becoming another Emmitt, as he told *HelloBeautiful.com*:

> When my father would say or do these things to me, I would hear this voice inside of me say, "That's not true" or, "Don't believe that" or "You're going to make it through this." I didn't know at the time what "it" was, but today I surely have no doubt that "it" was God.

That voice always gave me comfort. It allowed me to hold on. I wanted to commit suicide. It kept me from being a gangbanger or drug dealer. Worse than all of those things put together, it kept me from being [Emmitt]. It brought angels to comfort me after every foul, harsh word or every welt on my legs or back.

The physical pain was matched by the anger that controlled his emotions. Tyler carried that rage with him. Once a straight A student, it even caused him to be expelled three weeks before he was to graduate high school. The final straw was an argument he had with a school counselor that got him kicked out. Perry later attended night school and earned his diploma by passing his General Educational Development (GED) test.

Tyler had virtually no direction in life in his late teens. He was still living with his parents and fearing every moment with his father. Then fate stepped in. Tyler flipped on the television one afternoon and began watching *The Oprah Winfrey Show*. She and a guest were speaking about the therapeutic effects of writing a journal.

He felt motivated to take their advice. Aside from school projects, he had never written. He had little desire to start a journal. Tyler began writing letters to himself and developing fictional characters based on people in his life. He wrote about his experiences, but created new names because he did not want anyone learning about all he had been through. Writing gave him a sense of confidence and purpose. He later expressed to Winfrey the importance of gaining and cultivating that capability. He thanked her for providing the inspiration to begin escaping the past and start a new journey.

"I watched your show and you were speaking to me," he told her. "There was nobody around me that told me I could fly. Nobody at school, no teacher, nobody who said, 'You're special.' But I saw you on television and your skin was like mine. And you said, 'If you write things down, it's cathartic.' So I started writing. And it changed my life."

Perry became interested in plays. He did not have enough money to see live shows when they came through the Sanger Theater in New Orleans, so he devised a plan. He would wait until intermission, when patrons would leave to take a break, and sneak into their vacated seats. That would at least give him an opportunity to soak in the second half of live performances.

His life was changing. He still carried the anger and bitterness of his youth with him. He drifted from one job to another. He toiled as a carpenter's apprentice. He was inspired by a friend who read his writings and encouraged him to turn them into a play. He finally worked up the courage to change not only his name, but also his home.

Tyler Perry was about to take a roller-coaster ride to the depths of despair and to the heights of success.

Chapter 3

SEEKING HAPPINESS AND FULFILLMENT

Tyler Perry needed to escape. He did not want to leave behind every horrible reminder of the past because they provided inspiration for his new work as a playwright. He yearned instead to maximize his potential. So he packed his bags in the early 1990s and drove to Atlanta in his compact car.

Perry knew that the most populous city in the South was also a hot spot for African-American entertainment. Atlanta was a major stop in what had been known as the "chitlin circuit." The string of performance venues, named after the soul food chitterlings, provided black entertainers a chance to display their talents in the racially segregated South from the early 1900s well into the 1960s.

The civil rights movement brought changes to that part of the country, including integration of theaters. Times had changed dramatically well before Perry arrived there. But Atlanta was still racially divided geographically. Many African Americans remained in the inner city and struggled to survive financially. He targeted them when he conceived of creating a play based on his life experiences.

Some criticized the "chitlin circuit" for what they perceived as featuring stereotyped, low-class black characters. Perry embraced a different view. He gained tremendous respect upon learning of its history. He understood that it allowed black patrons banned from attending the same theaters as whites during many decades of segregation to support and promote black artists. Among those who performed in such theaters were legendary singers and musicians, such as Ray Charles, Billie Holiday, and Duke Ellington. Perry believed it still had a place in the African-American community years after the arrival of racial integration in the South.

The theme of his work centered on adult survivors of abuse. He considered it therapeutic to himself and to others. Knowing he could help other victims gave him a new sense of purpose. He also realized that his play could not aid those who still suffered from mistreatment in their youths if it was never produced.

Perry needed money to fund the project. While he honed his play, which he had by then titled *I Know I've Been Changed*, he worked odd jobs. He worked as a car salesman, hotel worker, and bill collector, which proved to be a valuable experience. He explained the benefits of that work to National Public radio interviewer Terry Gross. "If you can get the guy from Kentucky who is behind on his four-wheeler payment and the mortgage and everything else to send you a payment, you can negotiate a pretty good deal in Hollywood," he said.[1]

Perry was driven. *I Know I've Been Changed* was to be a Tyler Perry production from beginning to end. He planned to produce, direct, and even star in the play. He saved $12,000 to turn his dream into a reality. He threw every penny into producing it and renting out the 14th Street Playhouse, a small community theater with two hundred seats.

The play debuted in 1992. Perry expected to look out at the audience and see full houses for six performances. Instead, only thirty acquaintances showed up on opening night. The "run" of his play lasted one weekend.

He was devastated. He had not only lost his life savings on the flop but also job after job for taking time off to work on the play. He had no money for his rent or car payment. Every cent he planned to spend on bills was tied up in his investment.

Perry refused to give up. He took the play to different cities about once a year, but each one failed. He was out of money. He was able to afford the expense because someone in the audience always agreed to invest in two or three other shows.

Nothing worked. In 1992, Perry was even homeless for three months. All six-foot-five of him slept in his car, a tiny Geo Metro, parked in a hotel lot. He landed jobs in construction and used car sales. When he could afford rent, he lived in a tiny apartment in the seedy section of Atlanta and survived on the cheapest of food, such as Ramen noodles.

His mother had no faith in Perry succeeding in show business. She begged him to return home and find a job that would allow him to survive financially. Seven years had passed since Perry arrived in New Orleans. She believed her son had given his play long enough and that it had simply failed. Perry was beginning to believe that as well. He had hit bottom. He earned just enough money on side jobs to check into a pay-by-the-week hotel full of drug addicts.

In the cold winter of 1998, residents of the hotel started their cars every morning to warm them up. The fumes would waft through the window of his room. He would usually ask folks to move their cars, but he grew so despondent one morning that he simply laid on his bed and waited for the fumes to suffocate him.

However, he did not allow that to happen. He decided to get up and keep going. But he had also made up his mind to discard his dreams of becoming a playwright. He spoke about his decision during an interview for a feature about his life on the Biography Channel.

"At this time I had given up," he recalled. "I said I'm going to do like my mother said, find me a good job. If I could make five hundred dollars a week and get me some [health] benefits, that's what she wanted me to have."

However, something inside Perry motivated him to give his production one more chance. He took a different approach to marketing the project. He visited black churches around Atlanta and convinced their choir members and pastors to take prominent roles in the play. Perry staged the play at the House of Blues, an entertainment venue with various locations in big cities throughout the country. He was to take the starring part.

Perry made another bold gesture before the play opened. He called his father, who had abused him throughout his childhood. He yearned not to erase the haunting memories of the past but rather to end his emotional pain associated with those horrible times.

The two argued bitterly at first. They expressed their deepest, darkest feelings. The conversation proved to be a catharsis for both of them, as he explained in an interview with Oprah Winfrey. Perry recalled:

> He's yelling at me, cussing and screaming, and something happened to me. I started saying things I never thought I'd be able to—things I did not even know were in me. "How dare you? Who do you think you are? You are wrong." It was as if the little boy in me was screaming out everything he'd never been able to say. And my father is silent on the phone because he has never heard this side of me. And at the end of it, I hear him say, "I love you," which at the age of 27, I had never heard before.
>
> I hung up the phone and I knew something had changed. My entire source of energy had been ripped from me. From the time I'd left my father's house until that moment, I had been plugged into negativity. I was plugged into

anger to keep moving, to do the play, to work, to get up every day. It was based on [telling his father] . . . "I'm going to prove you wrong." But to this day, when I finally said those things, I had to find a new source of energy.

It was in that conversation that Perry told his father that he forgave him for all the cruelty and mistreatment. Hearing from his father that he loved him helped change his fortunes for the better. He felt a sense of peace. The negativity drained from his life. He did not want to forget his troubled past. He was simply able to use it to create a positive future for himself.

"I found out in life that everything that happens to you can work for your good if you let it," Perry said after he had gained wealth and fame. "No matter how bad, no matter how traumatic. For me, my turnaround came when I forgave my father for everything he did and I realized that everything that had happened had brought me to this position where I am now. And it's allowed me to be able to write these stories and develop these characters because had I not been through those situations I wouldn't have the experience to be able to do that."[2]

The experience about which Perry spoke would never have happened had he taken the advice of his mother and returned to New Orleans. Little could he have known that his life was about to change dramatically in Atlanta on March 12, 1998, as he prepared for another opening night of *I Know I've Been Changed*. After that evening, he indeed realized he had been changed.

Perry was shaken as he put on his makeup before the performance. He anticipated another box office failure. At that moment, Perry felt like he heard a loud and clear voice. He believed it to be the voice of God. The mystical experience would prove to be a turning point in his career and his life. He heard God tell him that He—not Perry—would let him know when his career as a playwright was over.

At that moment, Perry glanced outside the window. A line had formed around the block to enter the House of Blues. His show had sold out. It also sold out the next seven nights. The venue proved too small for the patrons clamoring to watch it. Perry moved the play to the Fox Theater in Atlanta and sold nine thousand seats over the course of a weekend. Promoters who had wanted nothing to do with *I Know I've Been Changed* were suddenly calling Perry with offers to stage it.

One reason for its success was his marketing efforts to black churches. This included using choir members in the play, which drew their friends, families, and fellow churchgoers to the production.

Another reason was the passion Perry put into it. He drew on his own life experiences and those of his family members to create the plotline, characters, and dialogue.

The play featured lead character Mary, who had been married and given birth to two children before she had even reached adulthood. She was emotionally immature and careless. She became dependent on drugs to relieve the pressure of raising her kids. Her drug use made her angrier. She took out her rage through verbal and physical abuse of her children. A husband who was abusive to his wife and kids worsened family life.

The work exposed new talented performers besides Perry. Soul musician Ryan Shaw dropped out of school to participate in the show, exploding onto the scene in *I Know I've Been Changed*. The play also featured future Grammy Award-winning vocalist Ann Nesby, who played a supporting role.

What made the play unique, however, was the humor that Perry injected within the deadly serious subject matter. That would prove to be a tremendously successful formula for the twenty-eight-year-old playwright during the rest of his career. He believed in the mix of comedy and tragedy to entertain and educate audiences. His childhood hero, Norman Lear, had done the same thing. That philosophy, as well as his deepening Christian faith, was confirmed by the sudden success of the play. *AMBERmag.com* Editorial Director Marcia A. Cole explained the attraction of humor in the Perry work in an interview with the Biography Channel.

"*I Know I've Been Changed* deals with child abuse, and Tyler Perry is showing the subject for what it is," she said. "But he's doing it through the medium of laughter and humor and laughter breaks the intensity of those serious subjects. Everybody likes to laugh."

That laughter was about to spread around the United States. Perry took the play to major cities throughout the country, including New York, Chicago, Philadelphia, Miami, Dallas, and Washington, D.C., over the next two years.

A *Washington Post* review cited its unique nature, claiming it could not be compared with any other play of its genre, calling it "on the whole" the most "well-produced Gospel show" they had "ever seen." The play attracted a huge African-American audience. Its popularity spread through word of mouth. Patrons who enjoyed it told friends and relatives in other cities in which it was to appear. That helped it sell out wherever it was staged.

Among the impressed patrons in Dallas was a black evangelist named T. D. Jakes. He approached Perry following the show. Jakes had written a book about a female survivor of abuse titled *Woman, Though Art Loosed!* Jakes yearned to adapt it into a play and asked Perry to head the production, which was first staged in 1999. It too was a hit. It followed the same tour path as *I Know I've Been Changed.* It grossed $5 million in just five months.

The financial success of the two plays pulled Perry out of poverty, just as the cathartic phone conversation with his father had torn him free from his emotional bondage.

Perry had earned enough money by 2000 to own a six-thousand-acre home outside of Atlanta. He designed the house with the help of his father. Perry's carpentry background had already helped him build sets for his plays that were far more elaborate than others that had been staged on the chitlin circuit.

He was on a roll, but he was open to new career paths and ideas. In 2000, he was inspired by a trip to the theater to watch a zany movie featuring African-American movie star Eddie Murphy titled *Nutty Professor II: The Klumps.* Murphy played multiple roles in the film, a box office smash that was also well received by critics.

Perry decided he wanted to produce a lighthearted comedy in which he could display his acting versatility. The result was a play that he wrote, directed, and starred in titled *I Can Do Bad All by Myself.* But in the spotlight of entertainment history, the play itself takes a backseat to a lead character Perry created that has defined his career.

Her name was Madea. And she would vault Perry to superstardom.

Chapter 4

THE BIRTH AND GROWTH OF MADEA

Tyler Perry understood in 2000 that the ideal role model for black comedic actors was Eddie Murphy. Murphy had been an entertainment icon since he came to fame on the cast of the TV skit show *Saturday Night Live* in the 1980s. He blossomed into one of the funniest and most well-respected movie stars of his generation.

So when Perry watched Murphy play two older female roles in the hit film *Nutty Professor II: The Klumps*, he decided to take on a woman's character as well. He donned a fat suit, a huge polka-dot dress, and a silvery white wig. The sight of him wearing such an outfit was funny enough considering his large frame and imposing height of six-foot-five. But when he belted out the voice of an old woman, the humor took on a new dimension.

Perry had created a character named Mabel Simmons for his musical play, *I Can Do Bad All by Myself*. The woman that became known as Madea was only slated to make a five-minute appearance. However, when the lead actress never arrived on show night, Madea was forced to remain onstage and assume the lead role.

Perry was unsure at first if he could pull off the difficult role. He peered at himself in the mirror before the show opened. "What the heck are you thinking?" he asked himself. He was not asking himself that for long. The launching of the Madea persona proved to be a stroke of genius. It soon transformed Perry from a highly successful playwright into one of the biggest stars in the entertainment world.

The attraction of Madea was far more than visual. It also extended well beyond comedy. She was particularly embraced by black patrons who could identify with her. Many of them had mothers, grandmothers, or aunts who looked or acted like her. Madea was loud and crass, but she was fearless in expressing her feelings. She boasted a strong moral compass. To many in the audience, she was not just a character on a stage or screen. She was a real person. She certainly was to Perry, as he explained in an interview with National Public Radio.

"I thought I'd imitate the funniest person I know, and she is exactly the PG version of my mother and my aunt, and I just loved having an opportunity to pay homage to them," he said. "She's a strong, witty, loving [woman] . . . just like my mother used to be. She would beat the (heck) out of you but make sure the ambulance got there in time to make sure they could set your arm back, you know what I mean? Because the love was there inside all of it. . . . That's why I think the character is so popular, because a lot of people miss that type of grandmother."

Black actress Lynn Whitfield, who worked with Perry in the film *Madea's Family Reunion* (2006), described the kind of woman with whom she identifies Madea in an interview with the Biography Channel. "That woman who's larger than life, who tells you exactly what she thinks, who has not a problem to snatch you up in the collar and set you straight," Whitfield said. "And who will give you the most encouragement and the biggest hugs of your life when you're down and out. That's Madea."

Perry had created a monster. He did not enjoy wearing the big, hot, uncomfortable fat suit and wig. Speaking extensively in the Madea voice strained his vocal chords. He planned to discard the character when *I Can Do Bad All By Myself* ran its course. But audiences loved her and wanted to see more.

In *I Can Do Bad All by Myself,* the new character gave a moral voice and new life to the old theme of a dysfunctional family using love and spirituality to work through abusive and unhealthy relationships. Madea played the role of a mother to a daughter going through a divorce and a grandmother to the children her daughter brought into the home. Madea worked in her own aggressive and humorous way to prevent strained relationships and jealousies from tearing apart her family.

I Can Do Bad All by Myself did not match *Nutty Professor II: The Klumps* as a pure comedy. Perry had no desire to divorce his work from the serious drama that defined his upbringing and the religious principles that allowed him to rise above it. *Forbes* magazine writer Brett Pulley explained his perception of Perry's motivation in a 2005 article.

"Perry . . . produces morality tales in which bad people get what's coming to them and good people triumph through faith," Pulley wrote. "With a parade of sinners, saints and jokesters, his 'dramedies' are filled with sex, betrayal, laughter and tears. He aims to capture the real-life challenges faced by his audience."

Perry later gave depth and history to the Madea character. He decided that Madea should be greatly influenced by her mother, just as he was by his. Perry understood that many African Americans learned about life from their mothers and other female role models. He wrote about the influence Madea's mother had on her in his book *Don't Make a Black Woman Take Off Her Earrings*. Perry wrote the book from Madea's perspective. Perry quoted Madea as saying:

> She told me a lot of things about life. I've tried to remember all of it and take it with me. She told me a lot about taking care of myself. "There ain't no man going to do something for you that you can't do for yourself. Get out there and make it happen for yourself."

> [E]very Madea gets her values and spirit from her mother. It was passed down. I thank God I had a good, strong one. It's a [lineage] that is passed down. You get the good things or you get the bad things. . . . This temper comes from my momma. The good, gentle side comes from her, too. But that one that don't take no stuff is one of those personalities that she had.[1]

Perry did not gain critical acclaim for his early work with Madea. He was not motivated to impress reviewers but rather to attract black audiences that had rarely or never been to the theater. His plays were considered lowbrow entertainment to many, including some in the African-American community. But they were hugely successful. They sold out weeks before they opened wherever they were staged.

That was especially true with his next play, which many consider his finest work ever. Perry wrote, directed, and starred as Madea in *Diary of a Mad Black Woman*. It took the American theater by storm in 2001. It featured Madea helping a friend named Helen overcome the emotional trauma of learning on her wedding anniversary that her husband Charles wanted a divorce so he could live with his mistress. Perry also played the role of Charles's father.

Madea again used a mix of compassion, anger, religion, and reason to guide those she loved out of emotional turmoil. In one scene, Helen lamented her belief that not only was her husband gone but so was the wealth that she enjoyed. Madea worked to regain Helen's confidence and hinted that there were legal means to gain access to his money:

Madea: "Yes, the man left you, but you still young. You're rich, you're beautiful."

Helen: "No, I'm not rich, Madea. Charles is rich."

Madea: "If the [ex-husband] got money, you've got money too. Hello!"[2]

Perry certainly had money. His wealth and fame were growing with every successful play. He also gained a reputation for a unique onstage style that engaged the audience. When an occasional straggler would arrive after a show began, he would sometimes leave his character and address the late patron in a joking manner.

He would also quite often stray from the script to ad-lib lines with his quick wit. He understood that the mostly urban black female audiences that packed the theaters were his lifeblood. He worked with passion to entertain them and lure them back. Making the crowd feel involved was one way to achieve that goal and show appreciation for their support.

Perry had earned enough money to begin construction on a new twelve-thousand-square-foot home outside Atlanta in 2002. That wealth did not come merely from ticket sales. He had emerged as one of the most astute businessmen in the entertainment world. He copyrighted and acquired ownership of every play he produced. He sent out e-mail messages to potential patrons about performances coming to their theaters. Perry also earned huge profits from mail-order purchases of his plays on video at twenty or twenty-five dollars apiece.

Fans could not get enough of Madea. Perry made her the centerpiece and title character of his next two plays, *Madea's Family Reunion* (2002) and *Madea's Class Reunion* (2003). Perry used the familiar themes of family, forgiveness, and overcoming physical, sexual, and drug abuse to spotlight Madea's ability to heal others emotionally. In the latter work, he also revealed a disturbing, wacky character named Willie Leroy Jones, who claimed to have twenty-seven people living in his head.

The strain of writing, directing, producing, and acting in plays eventually overwhelmed Perry. The physical and mental responsibility of playing Madea was in itself a huge burden. He wrote her out of his 2004 play, *Why Did I Get Married?* This was the first time in his career as a playwright that he did not appear onstage.

The plot revolved around family members and their friends who ask themselves and others the question that was the title of the play. The group explores modern relationships in an annual retreat.

Some humorous scenes featured a widower named Poppy, who spoke to the audience while he awaited the arrival of the others. He revealed that the cabin is dusty and that he must be the one who cleans it. He swiped a cloth on the table for two seconds, choked, and coughed as the dust flew, and then strolled to the nearby couch.

"That's enough . . . I'm tired," he proclaimed before plopping down as the audience roared with laughter.

The popularity of *Madea's Class Reunion* motivated Perry to write a spin-off play titled *Meet the Browns*, which was later transformed into a television series. The plot revolved around a family dealing with planning and executing a funeral for their 107-year-old father and grandfather. The arrival of new family members revealed issues of marriage and parenting that had become staples of Perry productions.

His plays had grown so popular that he had staged about three hundred live shows each year. In 2005, he estimated that thirty-five thousand people a week had attended at least one of them. By that time, he had sold more than $100 million in tickets, $30 million in videos, and $20 million in merchandise. His e-mail list included four hundred thousand fans.

Yet Perry could not maximize viewership for three significant reasons. His plays were staged mostly in the eastern half of the United States. They could only draw limited audiences as they toured from one theater to the next. And they were only attracting urban black patrons.

Perry yearned to take his work to the movie screen. There was just one problem—he was a virtual unknown in Hollywood. He approached studios about producing a film adaptation of *Diary of a Mad Black Woman,* which would introduce Madea to moviegoers.

Studios were insistent that he rewrite his work to tone down its religious message. One studio representative angered Perry with what he perceived as an insulting statement that lumped together the taste of all black moviegoers. He simply took his script and walked away.

Perry had gained an understanding over the years of the importance of maintaining creative control of his work. He did not simply want to entertain his audiences. He sought to express his message about family, forgiveness, and spirituality in film, just as he did onstage. He refused to give that up despite the potential of earning more money than he had at any point in his career. He was even prepared to spend $5 million of his own money to fund the movie project himself.

That did not become necessary. He hooked up with Lions Gate Films, a small studio that specialized in marketing to selected audiences. Lions Gate believed it could capitalize on the popularity of his plays in the black urban community. The studio was willing to take a chance that those same people that enjoyed

Diary of a Mad Black Woman and other Perry plays onstage would swarm to theaters to see the films.

Lions Gate and Perry split the cost of turning his dream into a reality. Perry had to fork over $5 million of his own money. But he considered the investment worth it because it allowed him to maintain creative control of the project.

"He who has the gold makes the rules," Perry later told *CBS News* correspondent Byron Pitts. "If someone is gonna give you the money, then they're gonna be in control. They're gonna own it, they're gonna tell you how it goes. They're gonna give you notes and give you changes. I wasn't willing to do that, so there was no other option for me."

Box office expectations were modest for the studio. Little did Lions Gate understand the attraction of Tyler Perry, as he explained in a Biography Channel interview. "I sat with the president of Lions Gate in a meeting before the movie opened," he recalled. "I said, 'What would you like to see the movie do?' He said, 'Well, if it does $20 million I'm happy.' I said, 'Opening weekend?' He starts laughing. He had no idea."

The success of *Diary of a Mad Black Woman* stunned Hollywood. The studio placed it in mostly urban African-American theaters to maximize patronage. Just as Perry predicted, it earned $21.9 million in its first weekend to grab the top spot among all new movie releases. Lions Gate President of Production Mike Paseornek was glowing in his assessment of Perry after the sales figures were announced.

"We have always believed that Tyler was a huge talent with enormous grass roots support," he said. "As this film continues to bring Tyler's heart, humor and immense popularity to a greatly expanded audience, it serves as a terrific platform for all of his work. . . . Tyler has introduced enduring and endearing characters to movie-going audiences nationwide that will have resonance for years to come."[3]

Critics were far less complimentary of the film and its creator. The clash between Perry and movie reviewers that had begun in his early years as a playwright intensified as his work hit the big screen. But nobody could argue that he was on his way to becoming a Hollywood star. Success in the world of television was also right around the corner.

Chapter 5

GRACING THE SILVER SCREEN

Financial success and critical success in film often coincide. Many movie patrons are driven to the theater by positive newspaper, magazine, and online reviews.

Such was certainly not the case with *Diary of a Mad Black Woman*, which was the first foray into filmmaking for Tyler Perry. The mainstream media universally panned the movie. *Chicago Sun-Times* critic Roger Ebert, who was perhaps the most respected and well known of his profession, believed the Madea character ruined what was potentially a good movie.

Ebert referred negatively to the scene in which Madea invaded the home of the man who was divorcing her granddaughter and began destroying furniture with a chainsaw.

"This touching story is invaded by the Grandma from Hell, who takes a chainsaw to the plot, the mood, everything," Ebert wrote. "A real chainsaw, not a metaphorical one. The Grandma is not merely wrong for the movie, but fatal to it—a writing and casting disaster. And since the screenplay is by the man who plays Grandma in drag, all blame returns to Tyler Perry. What was he thinking? There's a good movie buried beneath the bad one."

Ebert added his view that Madea "seems like an invasion from another movie. A very bad another movie. I've been reviewing movies for a long time, and I can't think of one that more dramatically shoots itself in the foot."[1]

Ebert later said he received more reaction from that review than any he had ever written. Those who embraced the film complained that Ebert did not understand the attraction of Madea to African-American audiences that identified with her as representing a strong older female figure in their own lives. Ebert replied in a column the following week that he would have preferred to see Madea in a comedy rather than as the lone comedic character in a drama such as *Diary of a Mad Black Woman.*

The presence of an outrageous character like Madea in serious dramas perplexed critics and others unfamiliar with Perry's work. His loyal urban black patrons did not perceive a problem. They thought of Madea as a humorous woman who used her passion and experience to solve the grave social issues of friends and family.

The poor critical response did not stop the film from earning more than $50 million at the box office. It did not prevent Black Entertainment Television (BET) from handing Perry two honors at its 2005 comedy awards show—Outstanding Writer in a Theatrical Film and Outstanding Actor in a Theatrical Film. Perry also won a Black Movie Award for Outstanding Achievement in Screenwriting.

The achievements of Perry as a playwright had allowed him to attract such notable actors as Kimberly Elise to play Madea's granddaughter and iconic veteran Cecily Tyson as Madea's daughter. Ebert praised both in his review. The success of the movie motivated other top actors to join new Perry projects. Tyson, respected actor Blair Underwood, Emmy Award-winner Lynn Whitfield, and legendary black poet Maya Angelou joined the cast of his next work, a film adaptation of *Madea's Family Reunion.*

The movie centered on the trials and tribulations of an African-American family that were played out at a reunion. Included among the characters were a woman physically abused by her fiancée, a juvenile delinquent, and a widow who sought to instill a sense of black pride in the younger generation. The movie featured stirring speeches from the Angelou and Tyson characters, as well as the zaniness of Madea.

Perry could not win the affections of critics, however, no matter how the moods of his films were skewed. A year to the day after Ebert complained that Madea ruined the drama in *Diary of a Mad Black Woman*, *New York Times* critic Anita Gates moaned in print that the drama wrecked a promising comedy that featured the Perry character.

"The commercials for Tyler Perry's film *Madea's Family Reunion* seem to promise a slapstick comedy about an obese black woman in late middle age who takes no guff and enjoys beating people up," Gates wrote. "It isn't exactly, and that's a disappointment. ... What the movie really needs is more of the fat lady throwing political correctness to the winds and slugging obnoxious adolescents. Very cathartic."

The growing legion of Madea fans agreed that Perry's movies needed more Madea. Her popularity was skyrocketing. *Madea's Family Reunion* earned $30 million in its opening weekend alone. Perry was far from a media star when he was producing plays. His venture into the movie industry brought him national attention.

It did not take much to set off rumors about Perry's personal life. When African-American supermodel Tyra Banks appeared at the premiere of *Madea's Family Reunion*, Perry was forced to insist to reporters that she was just a friend. They were spotted dining out together, and Banks began flying across the country to attend his plays from the front row. Perry was surprised to be the target of paparazzi, photographers who seek to catch celebrities doing anything perceived as newsworthy, sometimes in their most private moments.

Perry did not need unwanted intrusions to bring attention to his work. His movies and the Madea character had grown so popular that he decided to take her into a new world. Perry wrote a book titled *Don't Make a Black Woman Take Off Her Earrings: Madea's Uninhibited Commentaries on Love and Life* in 2006. It featured dozens of humorous observations and opinions from Madea's perspective, as written by Perry, on a myriad of subjects.

The book cover showed an angry Madea preparing to remove an earring, which Perry cited as a sure sign of a physical confrontation. But Madea did not express only anger in the book, which is at its core her replies to letters Perry received that were addressed to her. She showed an array of emotions in writing about love, marriage, parenting, and religion. She even gave beauty tips.

It becomes obvious when reading the book that Perry was expressing his own beliefs on a number of subjects through Madea. He criticized the new direction of youth culture, including the passion for hip-hop music. He railed against teen pregnancy, offering that teenage girls should take their time before having sex. He wrote about the importance of education. He even joked about the odd names some black parents had given their newborns in more recent times. According to Madea:

> I don't even know how to pronounce sixteen-year-old girls' names anymore. Where the [heck] are these names coming from? Lequisha and Aquanisha and Bonequida and Chaniqua. What the [heck] does all of that mean? Did somebody go back to Africa and find all these names under a bush?

> [P]lease, parents and parents to be, give your child a name that's respectable—that people will understand and not sit around trying to figure out even how to pronounce it. . . . Do you know by naming your child these crazy names,

you automatically give them a disadvantage? Imagine your child going to interview at a Fortune 500 company. The secretary comes out and says, "Marisa Jones, you're next. Ms. Stacey Evans, you're next." And then she says, "Aquanisha Laquita Brown, you're next."

The book was all about Madea passing out advice. Among her favorite topics were relationships. She gave strong opinions, mostly to women. She believed that they should not settle for just any man to date or marry. In the following passage, Madea offered that women must be directed by a sense of pride and control their own destiny:

All these women wondering why they go out on a date and the man ain't calling in three days, he's not calling when he says he's going to call— baby, it's really simple. The man ain't interested. If he wanted you, he'd call you. And all these women sitting saying, "We've been dating all these years, when are you going to marry me?"

If you've got a man saying to you, "We're going to marry one day," . . . do you know what he's doing? This may hurt your feelings, but I'm going to be really honest. He's just waiting to see what else is out there, if something better is going to come along. If nothing better comes along in the next few years, you may have a shot at marrying him. That's what he's telling you. Don't put up with that. You are worth more than that, honey.

Perry presented messages in his book specifically for African-American youth. They provided what he believed was a moral direction for young, urban African Americans. Among them was rejecting stereotyped differences between how white and black people talk or live their lives. He criticized those who believe speaking properly or wearing business attire, for instance, is "acting white."

He wrote: "Get off this white-black thing, just be! Education is a good thing no matter who you are. Bill Cosby . . . and Barack Obama—they've made us proud. So now it's acceptable to speak proper English and wear nice suits. So what we used to think was 'white' is changing. It's not trying to be white anymore. It's being smart. Knowing your potential. Being a good representative of your family, your community, and the race of people you come from."

Perry had taken a leap forward in the entertainment world in 2005 and 2006 by delving into film and book writing. The book landed on the *New York Times* Best Sellers List and remained there for four months. It was also voted Book of the Year at the 2006 Quill Awards.

Perry continued to produce plays with and without his signature character, including *Madea Goes to Jail* (2006). It was later transformed into a movie. While the book was being snatched up at stores and online, he had delved into the only medium he had yet to explore—television.

It was the perfect outlet for Perry, who considers himself a storyteller. He was intrigued with the notion of telling another story every week in a sitcom that did not feature Madea. He did not want a network dictating the content or direction of his show, so he shot ten episodes of a program titled *Tyler Perry's House of Payne* and spent $5 million to fund the project before even striking a deal with a network. His cast featured no established TV stars. It was a risky undertaking and unheard of in the television industry.

The sitcom revolved around the African-American Payne family, which made its home in suburban Atlanta. In the show, three generations lived in the same house. The differences between the generations lead to both drama and humor.

Tyler Perry's House of Payne was picked up by cable network TBS, which specialized in running modern sitcoms, including several that target African-American audiences. The network ran the ten pilot episodes to test the market. TBS was impressed enough by the high ratings to give Perry a one hundred-episode commitment for $200 million, an incredible sum for an unproven series.

Perry served as a writer and director for the show. Its premiere attracted the biggest audience for any cable sitcom that week with an estimated 5.2 million viewers. All one hundred episodes were filmed over a period of just nine months, which allowed the sitcom to go quickly into syndication. The savvy Perry understood that syndication translates into wider distribution of programs and larger profits.

But Perry had certainly failed to win over the critics. The mainstream media panned the sitcom for what was perceived as lacking in humor and promoting black stereotypes. *USA Today* reviewer Robert Bianco was perhaps the most critical. He authored a scathing review of *Tyler Perry's House of Payne* in 2007:

> Well, at least the title's apt. Indeed, if ever a show could cause actual physical pain, TBS' *House of Payne* might be the one. Glaringly, shamefully, insultingly inept, this new cable comedy from filmmaker Tyler Perry isn't just the worst sitcom of the year. It's one of the worst in the modern era.
>
> And what's worse, you have to imagine the people at TBS know how terrible the show is, and they are proceeding nonetheless. The other

option—that they really think this horrendous mish-mash of old jokes and ugly stereotypes fills some TV void—is too hideous to contemplate.

Millions of fans did not agree with the negative reviews. The success of the show and past triumphs allowed Perry to afford a seventy-five-thousand-square-foot studio in Atlanta to produce all his projects. His desire to work at a feverish pace left little time for his personal life. His relationship with Banks had grown more serious but ultimately failed because both were married to their work. Perry believed his future included a wife and children. However, he knew he could not be a good husband or father until he had more free time.

He certainly had little free time in 2006, which he finished by writing and directing a movie titled *Daddy's Little Girls*. The first Perry film without Madea centered on a strong black father figure named Elba, an auto mechanic who was seeking to maintain custody of his three daughters from his unfit ex-wife. The cast featured Academy Award-winning actor Louis Gossett, Jr., who played Willie, the owner of the shop in which Elba worked.

Daddy's Little Girls received stronger reviews than Perry's previous films, especially from those who railed against the Madea character. He was credited for his casting of the main characters in the movie but condemned again for a perceived stereotyping of African Americans.

Perry, however, showed a strong sense of black history in writing the movie. The shop Willie owned and in which Elba worked was on Auburn Avenue in Atlanta. The street has historical significance in the world of African-American entertainment and in the civil rights movement of the 1950s and 1960s. It housed a hotel above a theater in which African-American acts stayed and performed. It was also the birthplace of legendary civil rights leader Martin Luther King, Jr., and the current home of the King Center, the official memorial for Dr. King, which educates the world about his life and his philosophy of nonviolence.

Perry asked Gossett to write a speech for the film that Willie delivered to members of the black community on Auburn Avenue. Gossett expressed his appreciation for that opportunity in a Biography Channel feature about Perry. "Willie is an elder," Gossett explained. "He's seen history change in his lifetime. It's very, very African, very African-American, and very necessary for us to reconnect with those generations to get the wisdom and have a baton to pass on. Tyler wonderfully knows that in his stories."[2]

Black female actors also praised Perry for creating positive images of African-American women through his films. It was a conception of women that was nurtured during his childhood as he spent valuable time with his mother and aunt. Perry saw them as the backbone and moral foundation of his family and sought to portray women as such in his movies. Actor Kimberly Elise spoke about her feelings in the same Biography Channel feature.

"I definitely feel like Tyler is consciously making a choice to elevate us as black people in the availability of images and emotion for black audiences that have been neglected for so long. I can say without hesitation that he is the only person I can think of who is actively creating leading roles for black actresses."

Yet a perception of black stereotyping was to become a common criticism of Perry as he emerged as one of the most versatile figures in American entertainment. Soon his work would draw anger from some of his fellow African Americans in the industry. Perry was proud of his achievements and the portrayals of black characters he created. He eventually felt compelled to express his resentment to those who condemned him.

Chapter 6

CONTROVERSY AND CRITICISM

Tyler Perry wanted to be done with Madea by 2007. There was just one problem—her fans wanted to see more of the wacky, pistol-packing character.

Perry was ready to retire the wild woman of his plays and early movies. She was nowhere to be seen in his next project, a film adaptation of his 2004 play, *Why Did I Get Married?* Rather than don the uncomfortable fat suit and wig and raise his voice to play Madea, he embraced the role of a pediatrician named Terry who was in a confrontational relationship with his wife.

The movie featured four couples struggling in their marriages who get together in a Rocky Mountain retreat. Perry strayed from themes he had spotlighted in plays and films that featured Madea. The couples sought to overcome infidelity or work-related problems rather than drug addiction or physical abuse.

Among the featured actors was star singer Janet Jackson. Her presence helped attract more moviegoers, reducing the risk of not including Madea in the script. *Why Did I Get Married?* opened at number one at the box office despite the absence of the beloved character. The addition of the popular Jackson to the cast attracted a greater number of white patrons than typically attended Perry films.

New York Times critic Jeannette Catsoulis believed after soaking in the movie that Perry was getting the hang of film writing and directing. She appreciated that Perry toned down the preachy, religious tone of earlier works to create more depth to his characters.

"Gone, along with Madea's (wildness), are the thundering gospel ballads and revivalist atmosphere," Catsoulis wrote. "In their place is a beautifully shot, fluid drama filled with compassionately written characters. Though still a stranger to subtlety, Mr. Perry has learned to balance the obviousness of his setups with characters whose interactions feel genuine."

He had learned to balance his many talents long before that. Perry continued to display his versatility in 2008. He directed, wrote, produced, and starred in the film adaptation of *Meet the Browns* and a new movie titled *The Family That Preys Together*. He handled all the same roles aside from acting in a play titled *The Marriage Counselor* that was brought to the silver screen four years later.

Perry continued to attract the premier actors for his movies. Golden Globe-winner Angela Bassett starred as a mother who accompanied her children to meet their father's family after his death in *Meet the Browns*. The film was turned into Perry's second television series a year later. Academy Award-winner Kathy Bates was cast as a woman trying to heal the emotions of loved ones in *The Family That Preys Together*.

One might wonder how Perry found time to sleep and eat. The workaholic also had a thirty-thousand-square-foot dream home built in the ritzy Atlanta section of Buckhead. He began construction of a larger studio that covered fifty acres and two hundred thousand square feet.

Perry focuses with great intensity on one project at a time. He rises at 5:30 A.M. for a workout, during which he thinks about the upcoming task. During the course of the day, he remains in tune to what he calls

"God's voice," though he admits it is difficult to hear over the din of all his activities. That leads him to take time off in the middle of the day to be alone in his office with his thoughts. He keeps a journal to record any ideas that inspire him. He takes pride in staying focused on creating the best movie, play, or television show possible. He understands that even though he is working with hundreds of people at a time, it is his name and reputation that are on the line.

It appeared that the only pursuit he did not find time for was dating—but appearances can be deceiving. Perry was still traumatized by the sexual abuse he experienced as a child. He found it difficult to enjoy intimacy with a woman. On one occasion, a woman clicked a door shut as a prelude to what she believed was to be an intimate encounter with Perry. Another woman wore lingerie in the same situation with him. Certain triggers caused Perry to relive the abuse he faced as a child, making him uncomfortable with women in intimate situations.

In December 2009, the death of his mother motivated Perry to come to grips with his past and work to overcome the psychological and emotional effects of the childhood abuse. He had forgiven his father long ago. He learned to separate himself from the despicable acts of others. He finally expressed his inner feelings a year later in an interview with media mogul Oprah Winfrey. He spoke about how he never wanted to tell his mother all he was going through emotionally when she was alive. He believed she had been through enough. Perry said:

> She suffered so much horror in her life—surviving breast cancer, the abuse from my father, the belittling, the beatings. And I just could not be a source of pain. I knew if I spoke about this, that she would be hurt. So I didn't. . . . I feel this tremendous sense of, "Now it's time for me to take care of me and get some of this stuff out of me and be free from it."

> All these [abusers] had given me something to carry. I think that everyone who's been abused, there is a string to the puppet master, and they're holding you hostage to your behaviors and what you do. At some point, you have to be responsible for them. What I started to do is untie the string and chase them down to where they came from. And I was able to free myself and understand that even though these things happened to me, it was not me.

While Perry worked out his personal issues, he continued to maximize his professional potential. *Meet the Browns* had joined *Tyler Perry's House of Payne* on cable network TBS and had similar success.

More than 4 million viewers tuned into its debut in January 2009. It became the top-rated sitcom on the station by March 2010. It was the number one scripted series on all of television for African-American audiences ages eighteen to forty-nine.

Perry also realized he could not bury Madea. Fans clamored for her return. In 2009, she appeared again on the big screen in film adaptations of *Madea Goes to Jail* and *I Can Do Bad All by Myself* and on the stage in *Madea's Big Happy Family* (2010).

Madea Goes to Jail earned a whopping $41 million in its first weekend—the largest opening of any Perry film to date—but received mixed reviews. Some critics offered that it was Perry's best Madea film. Others believed Madea was holding him back from creating better work. *New York Times* reviewer A. O. Scott saw both sides, indicating that fan passion forced Perry to return Madea to the movie theaters.

"There is something both satisfying and frustrating about 'Madea Goes to Jail,'" Scott wrote. "[M]r. Perry dutifully gives his audience what it wants, but you can't help feeling that he might also have more to offer: more coherent narratives, smoother direction, better movies. Still, as long as he had Madea—force of nature and now something of a pop-culture institution—he might not need any of that."

He also did not need the backlash against Madea, as well as his plays and films, from others in the African-American entertainment world. Academy Award-nominated director Spike Lee was his harshest and most respected critic. He began a war of words with Perry by claiming his TV comedies brought back the days of pervasive negative stereotypes of African Americans in the media.

Lee voiced his criticism to interviewer Ed Gordon on a television show *Our World With Black Enterprise*. He criticized not only Perry but also the African Americans who watched his movies and shows, which he compared to the absurd depictions of African Americans in the media from the 1920s to the 1950s. He specifically mentioned a 1930s and 1940s comedian named Mantan Moreland, whom he felt fed negative stereotypes.

"A lot of this is on us," Lee said. "You vote with your pocketbook, your wallet. You vote with your time sitting in front of the idiot box, and [Tyler Perry] has a huge audience. . . . But at the same time, for me, the imaging is troubling and it harkens back to 'Amos n' Andy.'

"Each artist should be allowed to pursue their artistic endeavors, but I still think there is a lot of stuff out today that is coonery and buffoonery [negative black stereotyping and silliness]. I know it's making a lot of money and breaking records, but we can do better."[1]

Black author Tom Burrell agreed, but he too did not place all the blame on Perry. He cited the 2008 film *Meet the Browns* in pointing the finger at black audiences in his book *Brainwashed: Challenging the Myth of Black Inferiority*.

"It's not entirely fair to expect Perry to chart a new course alone," Burrell wrote. "His movies and TV shows would not be so successful if blacks didn't have a raging appetite for messages and images that project us as dysfunctional or incompetent. Nothing that occurred during Amos 'n' Andy's radio and television reign could match the words and actions of black comedies like Madea and The Browns. Our attraction to self-demeaning images came way before, and goes far beyond, Tyler Perry."

Others argued that Madea and other characters in Perry's plays and films were a real representation of people that urban African Americans have known in their lives. They further contended that Madea, in particular, provided a moral direction to young, impressionable African Americans in a comedic way.

Perry became irate at the criticism. He argued that such views expressed by Lee prevented films and television shows from being produced for the tastes of urban African Americans. Perry defended his work during an interview on the news show *60 Minutes* in October 2009.

"I would love to read that [criticism] to my fan base," he said. "That [angers] me. It is so insulting. It's attitudes like that, that make Hollywood think that these people do not exist, and that is why there is no material speaking to them, speaking to us. . . . All the characters are bait—disarming, charming, make-you-laugh bait. I can slap Madea on something and talk about God, love, faith, forgiveness, family, any of those."

Perry found a powerful ally in the black community in the universally respected Oprah Winfrey. She had gained tremendous success in the entertainment world and had devoted much time to promoting positive black role models. She told *New York Daily News* reporter Issie Lapowsky that Madea and other Perry-created characters were a reflection on the uplifting forces of his upbringing.

"I think [Perry] grew up being raised by strong, black women," Winfrey said. "And so much of what he does is really a celebration of that. I think that's what Madea really is: a compilation of all those strong black women that I know and maybe you know too? And so the reason it works is because people see themselves."

The National Association for the Advancement of Colored People (NAACP) also sided with Winfrey in her support of Perry. The civil rights organization was shocked and thrilled when Perry donated $1 million to celebrate its 100th anniversary. Perry planned to distribute the gift over the course of four years.

The NAACP presented Perry with its Chairman Award in recognition of "special achievement and phenomenal public service." Perry was in elite company. The honor had been presented to President Barack Obama among other luminaries. The NAACP was motivated by Perry's charitable efforts, including his donation of $110,000 and a new van to an Atlanta homeless shelter.

Highly respected civil rights leader and NAACP Board Chairman Julian Bond made the selection of Perry as the Chairman Award winner. He released a statement announcing the motivation for his decision.

"Tyler Perry is a tremendous inspiration to people on many levels," it read. "His remarkable life experiences, which inform his extraordinary body of work in film, television and stage, have also shaped his focus on significant charitable causes and civil-rights initiatives."[2]

Nobody could accuse Perry of supporting negative black imagery as a coproducer of the 2009 film *Precious*. The film revolved around an obese New York City teenager who fantasized of a better life. She used her determination to overcome physical, sexual, and emotional abuse. It was among the most highly acclaimed movies of the year and a surprise hit.

Precious earned more than $63 million at the box office. It won Academy Awards for Best Performance by an Actress in a Supporting Role (Mo'Nique) and Best Writing. It was also nominated for Best Motion Picture of the Year, Best Film Writing, and Best Performance by an Actress in a Leading Role (Gabourey Sidibe).

Perry was also not about to retire Madea, despite serious pressure from some in the African-American community. She returned to the big screen in the 2009 film adaptation of *I Can Do Bad All by Myself*, which he also wrote and directed. But Madea had a far less substantial role in the movie than she did in the play of the same name that had hit the stage nine years earlier.

The film was also noteworthy for its casting of singers Gladys Knight and Mary J. Blige. Thanks to those soul superstars, it proved to be the first adaptation of a Perry play to feature as much singing as the stage production. Entertainment magazine *Variety* critic Peter Debruge gave the movie a lukewarm review in which he claimed it was too predictable.

"There are absolutely no surprises in store, plot-wise, though Perry's approach has always been to rework familiar narrative conventions in such a way as to reaffirm key values (namely, generosity, community and forgiveness), remind us that no hardship is too severe to overcome . . . and supply laughter . . . in hearty doses," Debruge wrote.

That is all Perry ever attempted to do. His goal was to humor and send inspiring, positive messages to a loyal audience. He was growing as a writer, director, and producer. He continued to explore all avenues in his professional career.

He was looking forward. He did not want to look back. But one day he returned to his old neighborhood in New Orleans as part of a national television biography about his life. The journey brought back all the haunting memories of a childhood filled with emotional and physical pain.

Chapter 7

HELPING OTHERS, HELPING HIMSELF

I t was the heat of the summer in 2010. Perry was strolling through his old New Orleans neighborhood with *CBS News* correspondent Byron Pitts. The cameras were rolling. Perry was being interviewed for a feature about his life on the legendary news show *60 Minutes*, which had been a staple of Sunday night TV programming in America for more than forty years.

They visited the house in which he once lived. Perry's heart was racing. Terrible memorics flooded back to him. He recalled the beatings from his father. He felt the emotional and physical pain all over again.

He experienced good recollections as well. He and Pitts met two women neighbors who reminded him of Madea, the character that provided him wealth and fame.

"Christian women with guns," Perry joked. "And the people wonder where Madea came from!"

Perry had forgiven his father. But his dad had never apologized for the mistreatment of his son. Perry revealed in an emotional message to his fans in 2009 that he was working to overcome terrible abuse meted out by Emmitt Perry, Sr. He wrote about the power of forgiveness. The gesture had him expecting a call from his father. He believed the man who tormented him would call him to express regret for his actions.

Quite the opposite happened. His dad never called. He simply sent a message through Perry's brother stating, "If I had beat your [butt] one more time, you probably would have been Barack Obama."[1]

Those words did not help Perry heal his emotional wounds. However, they did not prevent him from taking care of his father financially. He continued to send him a check every month, which allowed him to live in a sprawling mansion in Louisiana.

Perry believed that since he had forgiven his father years ago, he had to provide for his welfare. He refused, however, to have a relationship with his father. He understood that without the apology, the emotional pain could never be erased when they were together.

He did not only heal by avoiding his father. He healed through helping others—and not simply through planned charities, such as his work with at-risk and disadvantaged youth and victims of AIDS, homelessness, and sexual abuse. Perry sometimes gave of himself spontaneously.

In late 2010, he learned that the home of an eighty-eight-year-old great-grandmother in Atlanta had burned to the ground. She and her four-year-old great-granddaughter had barely escaped the blaze. Firefighters began a campaign to raise money. Soon, the community had built her a new house. Perry, however, yearned to do more. He visited the woman and pledged to pay her rent and utilities for a year and buy her a new, furnished home. His generosity proved to be a pleasant surprise for the great-grandmother, her great-granddaughter, and the Atlanta firefighters.

"It made my Christmas," fire chief Todd Moore told the media. "I've been doing this a long time, seen a lot of bad things come and go but this is special."[2]

So was Perry's ability to make money. He had maintained his status as one of the most successful entertainers in the world in 2010. Five of his eight movies had opened number one at the box office, which could not be said about such famed directors as Steven Spielberg and Quentin Tarantino. His movies had combined to gross more than $418 million, the highest per-film average in Hollywood.

Nothing was about to change that year either. Perry produced, directed, and starred in *Why Did I Get Married Too*, a sequel to his 2007 movie. The film featured the same four couples embarking on a vacation retreat, this time in the Bahamas, where they worked to improve their strained relationships.

The movie delved into grave issues such as infidelity, unemployment, incurable illness, and dealing with the death of loved ones. *USA Today* critic Claudia Puig offered that the script did not live up to the importance of those subjects.

"While the message is a worthy one, the story Perry tells to illustrate it lacks any subtlety," she wrote. "There's no shortage of yelling, ranting, sobbing or objects being thrown. At the same time, serious issues are trotted out, some glossed over and others left hanging. Twists and coincidences are thrown in for forced shock value. . . . Most of the scenarios devolve into trite formula."

The film earned more than $30 million in its opening weekend and $60 million overall despite the mediocre reviews. Perry had cemented his core fan base of urban, churchgoing African Americans, many of whom were women. Those who embraced Madea were soon to get their gift as well. She was front and center in the play *Madea's Big Happy Family* (2010), which returned the central character to the stage for the first time in four years.

His plays were big business. So many fans sought tickets to his plays that they were forced into larger venues. Thousands of patrons poured into one 2010 show at the Arco Arena in Sacramento, California. Included were several stars of the Sacramento Kings NBA basketball team.

Perry plays were also more polished than ever. His sets were elaborate. He was casting veteran actors who had gained familiarity with his work. He also sought to engage his audiences. He still ad-libbed lines and even stopped his shows to speak to the audience or make them laugh with a joke not in the script. Theatergoers sang along to the music, which ranged from gospel to rhythm and blues. Perry would then speak to audiences after the show, explaining that the Madea character was based on his mother.

Madea indeed remained fresh and funny to her fans. The sight and sounds of the hulking Perry onstage in a white wig, outdated glasses, and huge blue polka-dot dress while belting out threats in the voice of an old woman induced laughter. *Sacramento Press* critic Jonathan Mendick offered that he was thoroughly entertained by the 2010 show in his city. He cited both the humorous and solemn subjects and praised Perry's writing and character development.

"For every comic element, there seems to be a serious moment as well," he wrote. "The play deals with issues like religion, drugs, and rape. The moral of the play, given to a dying grandmother to her family is, 'If you're loving real love, then you've lived life.'

"The characters have surprising depth during serious parts of the play, but the comic elements remain slapstick. At one point, Madea slaps a drug-dealing young father and chokes his girlfriend for being stupid."

Such wacky comedy was typical of what Perry had been writing and producing since he created Madea a decade earlier. The attraction of his work had branched out little beyond urban African Americans, particularly women. But Perry was changing. He yearned to give his work a universal, intellectual appeal. The result was the November 2010 release of his movie *For Colored Girls*.

Perry wrote, directed, and produced the film adaptation of the highly acclaimed 1975 play titled

For Colored Girls Who Have Considered Suicide When the Rainbow Is Enuf. At the time, the play was considered an important piece of black literature and a reflection of the emerging black feminist movement in the United States.

For Colored Girls focuses on the lives of nine African-American women struggling with such issues as abandonment, abortion, and rape. Many of the finest black singers and actors were motivated to lend their talents to the movie, including Janet Jackson, Whoopi Goldberg, Phylicia Rashad, Kimberly Elise, and Kerry Washington.

The film earned financial success, bringing in $20 million in its first weekend. Mainstream and consistent critical praise still eluded Perry, however. Reviewers enjoyed the acting performances but panned the overall production.

Black intellectuals in the entertainment world also continued to condemn Perry in 2011. Further criticism by Spike Lee inspired Perry to offer that his fellow filmmaker could "go straight to hell." Those words inspired more debate. In an interview with National Public Radio, culture critic Touré and journalist Goldie Taylor argued about whether Perry had lowered the standards of entertainment for millions of black patrons or provided a fair representation of urban African-American people and life.

Touré was highly critical of Perry, calling him "perhaps the worst filmmaker in Hollywood." He went on to complain that Perry had no business firing back in a war of words against Lee.

"I think there's definitely a divide between the people who just like the spiritual messages, seeing some black people on screen, and others of us who, when we go to the movies, we want to see more," Touré said. "We want to see transcendent filmmaking. Tyler's title 'I Can Do Bad All by Myself' is an excellent title for him because he does do bad all by himself. He should only mention Spike Lee's name with reverence. Spike is the best black filmmaker of his generation."

Taylor gave quite a different view. "What I applaud a Tyler Perry for doing is taking very relevant, important things that some other filmmakers are just too afraid to touch and touch them in a special way that meets his audiences at his point of need," she said. "I don't think Tyler is talking to me, but I know that he's speaking directly to my mother, my sister, my cousins and meeting them at their point of need, and that's what art and filmmaking is about."

Asked what she meant by "point of need" Taylor continued. "What I mean is that when women are talking about their own sense of brokenness, whether it is themes about . . . domestic violence or joblessness or who we choose as mates, these kinds of very hard themes that Tyler has begun to paint the picture differently," she said. "And I think that when my mother and sister and cousins watch this stuff, they see a bit of a reflection of themselves, of their neighbors, of their sisters and friends."

The debates over the merits of Perry's work seemed unending. But so did his success. He adapted his *Why Did I Get Married?* plays and movies into a third television series, titled *Tyler Perry's For Better or Worse* in 2011. Perry wrote, directed, and produced the show. It was equal parts drama and sitcom. It featured the familiar Perry themes of couples struggling to make their relationships work.

Its Friday night launch on TBS attracted 3.4 million viewers and ranked number one among all basic cable television programs in November. Its debut and new episodes of *Tyler Perry's House of Payne* combined to make TBS the most-watched cable network in prime time among all adults ages eighteen to forty-nine.

He was as hot as ever professionally. And soon he would experience something in his personal life he had been seeking for many years—love. Perry announced to *Sister2Sister* magazine publisher Jamie Foster-Brown in early 2012 that he had fallen deeply in love with a woman rumored to be Ethiopian model Gelila Bekele, whom he had dated previously.

Perry admitted that his appearance on *The Oprah Winfrey Show* in 2010, in which he spoke about the sexual abuse he endured in his childhood, allowed him to open his heart to a woman. But he was secretive about the relationship and planned to remain so. He declined to confirm or deny reports that they were engaged and planning a huge wedding.

"I will be married and probably have kids before anybody knows it," he said. "I'm very much in love. And she loves me. I don't talk about it."

What Perry did want to talk about was his movies. He directed, wrote, produced, and acted in all three of his 2012 films. The first was *Good Deeds*, in which he played the role of a wealthy businessman and fiancé whose life was turned upside down when he met an attractive female janitor in his office. He was torn between remaining loyal to his fiancée and having an affair with the janitor, a single mother who had been evicted from her apartment.

Perry tried several risky new approaches when he brought *Madea's Witness Protection* to the big screen. It was his first release in the highly competitive summer season. It dealt more with financial misdeeds rather than the emotional issues more typically spotlighted in his work. It was the first film with Madea that did not debut onstage. And it was his first movie that featured a largely white cast.

He had for years depended on black patrons that had seen his plays to pack movie theaters for film adaptations. That did not stop *Madea's Witness Protection* from earning a whopping $65 million at the box office. It was the second-highest grossing film ever for Perry, behind *Madea Goes to Jail*.

Perry, who had stepped away from his usual versatile role in filmmaking by taking only an acting part in the 2009 hit movie *Star Trek*, did so again in the 2012 film *Alex Cross*. Perry played a small role in *Star Trek*, however. He starred in *Alex Cross*, which proved to be a departure. The movie was a crime thriller that cast Perry as a psychologist and homicide detective. In the film, a serial killer tested his character morally and physically.

The movie was universally panned. But critics were no more critical of the performance of Perry than the rest of the production. *Los Angeles Times* reviewer Betsy Sharkey claimed that he simply needed to find a better film in which to display his talents. She added that falling back on the series of Madea movies was also not his best choice.

"The best of the 'Alex Cross' mess suggests that as an actor, he has the talent to move beyond the world of Madea should he want to," Sharkey wrote. "He just needs to look for much better material."

Millions of Perry fans were convinced that the Madea movies were fine material. They were not about to apologize for it. Others, including some African Americans in the show business world, complained that films featuring Madea represented the worst in black entertainment. Still, others believed his only worthy plays and films were those that featured Madea. It seemed Perry could not win the hearts and minds of anyone but his loyal fans.

Among those loyal fans was Oprah Winfrey. The media mogul wanted Perry on her team as a contributor to the cable TV station, the Oprah Winfrey Network (OWN). So in 2012, she signed Perry to produce, direct, and write a new television series for OWN. In February 2013, the network purchased new episodes of the Perry show *For Better or Worse*.

It seemed to be an ideal fit. Winfrey and Perry had a long history of mutual respect. Perry credited a Winfrey show that aired more than twenty years earlier for setting him on the path to becoming a playwright. He had also had a therapeutic session on her show in which he unburdened himself about the physical and sexual abuse he was forced to endure in his youth.

The television network had grown in popularity, especially among women in the 25–54 age group, in which Perry had thrived for many years. Winfrey spoke glowingly of Perry after the deal was struck.

The network had yet to delve into the world of scripted fictional programming.

"I have been looking forward to the day when we would be in the position to enter the world of scripted television," Winfrey said. "That day has come. We are all energized by the opportunity to celebrate with Tyler, who has a proven track record for producing highly successful cable series. He has an incredible ability to illuminate life stories and characters in his unique voice and inspires and encourages people all over the world."

No better argument for the talent of Tyler Perry and his value to the entertainment world had ever been spoken.

CHRONOLOGY

1969—Born Emmitt Perry, Jr., on September 13 in New Orleans, Louisiana, to mother Willie Maxine and father Emmitt, Sr.

1980—Experiences sexual abuse from mother of friend, one of several such incidents in his life.

1990—Moves to Atlanta, Georgia, after *The Oprah Winfrey Show* motivated career as a writer.

1992—First play *I Know I've Been Changed* flops at Atlanta community theater.

1998—Has cathartic phone conversation with father, forgives him for abusing him.

—Credits God for sudden success of play *I Know I've Been Changed*, which then moves to larger venue.

2000—Creates signature Madea character for the play *I Can Do Bad All By Myself.*

2005—First film *Diary of a Mad Black Woman* opens at number one in box office and is a smash hit.

2006—Perry writes, directs, produces, and stars in *Madea's Family Reunion*, which opens at number one at the box office on the weekend of February 24–26.

—A ten-show pilot of his first TV sitcom, *Tyler Perry's House of Payne*, debuts on cable network TBS in the spring.

—The popularity of Madea motivates Perry to write best-selling book titled *Don't Make a Black Woman Take Off Her Earrings*.

2007—Perry film *Why Did I Get Married?* released on October 12 proves to be hit at the box office and is eventually turned into a movie sequel and TV sitcom *Tyler Perry's For Better or Worse*.

2009—Second TV sitcom *Meet the Browns* debuts on TBS on January 7.

—*Madea Goes to Jail* is released on February 20 and becomes Perry's biggest box office hit.

—Black filmmaker Spike Lee criticizes Perry for promoting black stereotyping and Perry fights back verbally in October *60 Minutes* interview.

—Perry serves as executive producer of hit film *Precious*.

2010—Perry speaks about the abuse he experienced as a child in therapeutic interview on *The Oprah Winfrey Show* on October 20.

2011—Perry writes, directs, and stars in hit film *Madea's Big Happy Family*.

—Third sitcom *Tyler Perry's For Better or Worse* debuts on TBS.

2012—Perry announces he is deeply in love but declines to go into details about the relationship.

—Perry plays detective in film *Alex Cross,* which opens on October 19.

2013—Writes, directs, and produces the film *Temptation: Confessions of a Marriage Counselor.*

FILMOGRAPHY

Selected Films

2014: *Tyler Perry's Single Mom's Club* (Director, Producer, Writer)

2013: *Tyler Perry's A Madea Christmas* (Director, Writer, Actor)

2012: *Alex Cross* (Actor)

Tyler Perry's Madea's Witness Protection (Director, Producer, Writer, Actor)

2011: *Tyler Perry's Madea's Big Happy Family* (Director, Producer, Writer, Actor)

2010: *Tyler Perry's Why Did I Get Married Too?* (Director, Producer, Writer, Actor)

2009: *Precious* (Executive Producer)

Tyler Perry's I Can Do Bad All By Myself (Director, Producer, Writer, Actor)

2008: *The Marriage Counselor* (Director, Producer, Writer)

2007: *Tyler Perry's Daddy's Little Girls* (Director, Producer, Writer)

2006: *Tyler Perry's Madea's Family Reunion* (Director, Producer, Writer, Actor)

2005: *Tyler Perry's Diary of a Mad Black Woman* (Producer, Writer)

Television

2006–2012: *Tyler Perry's House of Payne* (Director, Producer, Writer, Actor)

2009–2011: *Tyler Perry's Meet the Browns* (Director, Producer, Writer)

2011–Present: *Tyler Perry's For Better or Worse* (Director, Producer, Writer)

2013–Present: *Tyler Perry's The Haves and the Have Nots* (Director, Producer, Writer)

2013–Present: *Tyler Perry's Love Thy Neighbor* (Director, Producer, Writer)

CHAPTER NOTES

Chapter 1: Forgiving, Not Forgetting

1. "Tyler Perry's Traumatic Childhood," *Oprah.com*, October 20, 2010, <http://www.oprah.com/oprahshow/ Tyler-Perry-Speaks-Out-About-Being-Molested-and-the-Aftermath/11> (March 27, 2013).

Chapter 2: Surviving Misery

1. "Tyler Perry videos," *Biography.com*, n.d., <http:// www.biography.com/people/tyler-perry-361274/videos/ tyler-perry-full-episode-2192392578> (March 27, 2013).

2. Deborah Bennett, "Tyler Perry Reveals History of Child Abuse & Molestation," *HelloBeautiful*, October 6, 2009, <http://hellobeautiful.com/515147/tyler-perry-reveals-history-of-child-abuse-molestation/> (March 27, 2013).

Chapter 3: Seeking Happiness and Fulfillment

1. "Tyler Perry Transforms: From Madea to Family Man," *NPR.org*, October 15, 2012, <http://m.npr.org/news/ Arts+%26+Life/162936803> (March 27, 2013).

2. "Watch I Know I've Been Changed Video," *VGuide. com*, n.d., <http://www.ovguide.com/i-know-i've-been-changed-9202a8c04000641f80000000047cb512#> (November 19, 2012).

Chapter 4: The Birth and Growth of Madea

1. Tyler Perry, *Don't Make a Black Woman Take Off Her Earrings: Madea's Uninhibited Commentaries on Love and Life* (New York: Riverhead Books, 2006), pp. 10–11.

2. "Tyler Perry's Why Did I Get Married Stageplay—Trailer," *YouTube,* April 17, 2012, <http://www.youtube.com/watch?v=I2vJaA_yRL8> (November 23, 2012).

3. "'Diary of a Mad Black Woman' Debuts at #1," Lions Gate press release, *Boxofficemojo.com,* February 27, 2005, <http://boxofficemojo.com/pr/?id=1737&p=.htm> (November 23, 2012).

Chapter 5: Gracing the Silver Screen

1. Roger Ebert, "Diary of a Mad Black Woman," *Chicago Sun-Times* online, February 25, 2005, <http://rogerebert.suntimes.com/apps/pbcs.dll/article?AID=/20050224/REVIEWS/50214001> (November 25, 2012).

2. "Tyler Perry videos," *Biography.com,* n.d., <http://www.biography.com/people/tyler-perry-361274/videos/tyler-perry-full-episode-2192392578> (March 27, 2013).

Chapter 6: Controversy and Criticism

1. Casey Gane-McCalla, "Spike Lee Compares Tyler Perry To Amos and Andy," *NewsOne: For Black America,* May 28, 2009, <http://newsone.com/191851/spike-lee-compares-tyler-perry-to-amos-and-andy/> (November 27, 2012).

2. "Tyler Perry to Receive Chairman's Award at NAACP Image Awards," NAACP press release, *Orlando Sentinel* online, February 1, 2010, <http://blogs.orlandosentinel.com/entertainment_tv_tvblog/2010/02/tyler-perry-to-receive-chairmans-award-at-naacp-image-awards.html> (November 28, 2012).

Chapter 7: Helping Others, Helping Himself

1. "Tyler Perry's Traumatic Childhood," *Oprah.com*, October 20, 2010, <http://www.oprah.com/oprahshow/Tyler-Perry-Speaks-Out-About-Being-Molested-and-the-Aftermath/11> (March 27, 2013).

2. "Tyler Perry to Build Fire Victims New Home," *wsbtv.com*, December 26, 2010, <http://www.wsbtv.com/news/news/tyler-perry-to-build-fire-victims-new-home/nFCYf/> (November 30, 2012).

GLOSSARY

box office—A term used in show business to describe an amount of money earned from a play or movie.

cast—A group of actors working on the same project.

catharsis—An experience that relieves tension or built-up negative emotions.

critic—A person who offers an opinion on any kind of performance.

director—Someone who supervises the making of a film, TV show, or play.

flop—A play or movie that fails financially.

luminary—A person who inspires or influences others.

patron—A person who attends a play or movie.

playwright—A person who writes plays.

premiere—The opening performance of a play or movie.

producer—A person responsible for the financial and administrative duties of any production.

refuge—A place a person goes to be alone and not bothered.

review—A written or spoken critique, usually of a movie, play, or TV show.

script—The written words and actions followed by actors.

sitcom—A form of TV entertainment known as a situational comedy.

staging—The performance of a play.

stereotype—A widely held but fixed and oversimplified image or idea of a particular type of person based on race, religion, sex, or physical characteristics.

studio—A place where movies are rehearsed and filmed.

syndication—To sell a program to independent television stations.

urban—Pertaining to an American city or town where people, often of lower economic status, live.

venue—A theater or any place where an entertainment event is held.

FURTHER READING

Books

Mattern, Joanne. *Tyler Perry*. Hockessin, Del.: Mitchell Lane Publishers, 2012.

Uschan, Michael V. *Tyler Perry*. Detroit: Lucent Books, 2010.

Internet Addresses

Biography.com: Tyler Perry
<http://www.biography.com/people/tyler-perry-361274>

Forbes: Tyler Perry
<http://www.forbes.com/profile/tyler-perry/>

IMDB: Tyler Perry
<http://www.imdb.com/name/nm1347153/>

INDEX